Real Estate Crowdfunding Explained

By Salvador Briggman

&

Krystine Therriault

http://www.crowdcrux.com

Introduction

I've watched the emergence and quick rise of real estate crowdfunding and I have to tell you, I've been dying to write this book. So many of my readers have reached out with questions about this growing new industry. Whether you are an investor, real estate developer, or entrepreneur, this new sector is a game changer.

My name's Salvador Briggman and I've been blogging about crowdfunding since 2012. On my main website, CrowdCrux.com, I bring awareness to crowdfunding success stories and demystify this alternative financial tool. I'm lucky enough to have impacted over 1 million website visitors in the past year and have been cited by the New York Times, Wallstreet Journal, and more.

In this ebook, my co-author Krystine Therriault and I bring tremendous clarity to real estate crowdfunding. We break down everything you need to know to get started raising money for a new property or investing in real estate online. Along with answering many of your questions, our biggest hope is that this comprehensive guide will get you pointed you in the right direction. We want you to succeed in this changing industry.

If you enjoy this ebook, please take a second to leave a review on Amazon or shoot me a message at sbriggman@crowdcrux.com.

Now...it's time to get ready to dive into the world of real estate crowdfunding!

- Sal

Table of Contents

Chapter 1: The Growing Real Estate Crowdfunding Industry

There's no marketplace so ripe for disruption as the real estate industry. With antiquated practices and a changing population demographic, this industry is on the verge of a total transformation.

In this section, we're going to cover the basics of this new sector and how it's changing the landscape for buyers, sellers, brokers, and institutions.

What is Real Estate Crowdfunding?

The best way to describe real estate crowdfunding (REC) is to explain how you can use it as an investor or real estate development firm. As an individual retail investor, you can invest in income-producing properties through a third party platform, known as real estate crowdfunding website. As a real estate development firm, you can get financing for a property fast on a secure online platform.

At its core, this platform serves as a marketplace for investors and developers. The entire transaction takes place online, making it much cheaper and more efficient than current financing routes.

But, it isn't all rainbows and sunshine in the real estate industry. Only five years ago, REC seemed far from possible. However, since the JOBS Act was passed in 2012, innovators from a number of different fields have come together and taken huge strides to build this industry into what it is today. With the SEC still working on regulations that will allow non-accredited investors to participate in equity crowdfunding, we'll probably be seeing even more growth in the next few years.

Like any other type of investment, real estate crowdfunding has its own unique benefits and drawbacks. If you're looking to get into REC as an investors or real estate developer, be prepared to do your homework! Although this book is a great starting guide, ultimately, you have to do your own research to figure out whether or not REC is right for you.

For example, currently, most REC platforms are limited to only accredited investors, except for a few platforms that are taking advantage of intrastate crowdfunding exemptions. This means that, as an investor, you must have a net worth over $1 million (excluding your primary residence) or an income of at least $200,000 per year (or joint income with a spouse exceeding $300,000) for the past two years in order to participate in this exploding industry.

In addition, most REC platforms focus on commercial real estate, such as retail properties, apartments, medical office space, etc (not ground up development). This might not be a great match for your development firm. However, some websites have recently seen success in funding single family homes, like Property Pool, Ground Breaker, and Patch of Land.

Throughout the rest of this chapter, we're going to define some of the key terms used in this industry, explain how the industry has progressed thus far, and give you an overview of the major platforms out there that you can use to finance real estate deals or get in on the ground floor as an investor in this growing marketplace.

Let's Define Some Key Terms and FAQ

Sponsor: In REC, a sponsor is the individual or company that is raising the investment to acquire and manage a real estate property. For almost every platform, they must have a strong history of real estate experience and the ability to manage the property and do due diligence.

Investor: Investors in REC deals are typically accredited investors or institutional investors who group together to make investments in exchange for either equity or debt.

Crowdfunding: When an individual or business raises money from a 'crowd' on a website or platform, rather than seeking out a single investors. Each campaign, opportunity, or project has it's own terms, goal, deadline, and minimum investment amount.

Crowdfunding platform: Most crowdfunding platforms are not brokers, advisors, or middle men. They provide the technology to facilitate an online marketplace of buyers and sellers. However, they may provide other services to sponsors and investors. Some sites will charge a fee to sponsors, investors, or both. Depending on the website, they may offer debt or equity capital deals.

How do platforms make money?

The way that platforms monetize varies from site to site. Some platforms will charge investors a fee, depending on the type of investment and transaction. Others will charge the sponsor a fee to list the property on their website. Some will charge both the sponsor and investor a fee to engage in the transaction. The platform or website may also have other premium services to support investors and sponsors. Finally, some real estate crowdfunding websites license their software so that other companies can host a private RE crowdfunding campaign or create their own platform.

What's the process to list your deal on a site?

First of all, it depends on whether you're going to be raising equity or borrowing money through the platform. Not every platform has debt financing. In general, you're going to be asked a variety of due diligence questions about your real estate firm and the nature of the opportunity.

Most platforms do not handle deals to develop a property from the ground up. Instead, platforms look for cash-flowing commercial properties and a proven real estate firm. Although the industry is new, an average raise can vary between $500,0000 and $5 million.

How do you become an investor?

At the time of writing, only accredited investors can join and invest on a real estate crowdfunding platform. An accredited investor is defined as:

1. Having earned $200,000 in the last two years OR a joint income of $300,000 in the last two years, with the expectation to continue earning at this amount.

2. Having a net worth that exceeds $1 million, individually or jointly with a spouse.

There are also entities that qualify for the accredited investor status, like banks and corporations. According to the SEC website, this is defined as "any trust, with total assets in excess of $5 million, not formed to specifically purchase the subject securities, whose purchase is directed by a sophisticated person, or any entity in which all of the equity owners are accredited investors."

If you qualify as an accredited investor, you can now join a platform and look at investment opportunities! Your minimum investment requirement will depend on the individual deal, but a requirement of $5,000 is average. Keep in mind that these investments are considered risky.

What's the difference between real estate crowdfunding and a REIT?

There are two main differences between real estate crowdfunding and a REIT.

First, on a real estate crowdfunding site, you'll be choosing the exact property that you want to invest in (location, specifications, etc). With a REIT, you'll be investing in a collection of properties of which you have no knowledge that were chosen by the REIT manager.

Second, since REITs are large corporations, it's unlikely that they'll be including smaller properties in their portfolio. On a crowdfunding site, you can invest in properties that are deemed to be "small investments," but that could have great returns!

There are some similarities. Like REC, REITs give investors a chance to diversify their income and own real estate without the hassle of actually maintaining the property. They do this by investing in portfolios of large-scale properties in exchange for equity or mortgage-backed securities.

However, REITS are much easier to liquify and investments in this asset class are known to increase in value over time. Almost all taxable income from these projects is passed along to shareholders as dividends.

On the flip side, rising taxes and falling occupancy can effect revenue and returns. REITs are a convenient form of passive income, but not great for people who want to be more in control with their investments.

Ultimately, crowdfunding focuses on the 'crowd' and gives you more power to choose what projects you want to invest in. Crowdfunding also opens up opportunities for niche investments that didn't exist before.

When will you get a return on your investment?

It's important to emphasize that these are risky and illiquid investments. Returns and distributions are subject to the timetable, milestones, and schedule of each individual listing. It's likely that you'll receive any distributions quarterly for equity investments, but it depends on the individual deal. Debt-based deals may distribute on a monthly basis. With regards to the overall return, there is no real secondary market for REC shares aside from other investors who have joined the deal.

How are investments structured?

This is a tricky question. It really depends on the REC platform. As mentioned previously, some platforms offer equity-based deals and others also offer debt-based deals. In addition, there is what's called "direct investing" and "in-direct investing." Direct investing is when you, as an investor, interact directly with the sponsor. The REC simple acts as an intermediary. Indirect investing is when you, as an investor, deal with the REC rather than sponsor. The platform acts as a single limited partner or lender that exclusively interacts with the sponsor.

How big is the REC industry?

Real estate crowdfunding has come a long way since the first projects were launched in 2012. In 2014, Fundrise's first crowdfunded property (Maketto, on H Street in Washington, DC) earned investors their first dividend check. That project raised $350K from 175 people at $100 per share. Now, about four years later, Fundrise is "doing a project a week and raising probably half a million dollars a day," according to co-founder Ben Miller (CNBC).

The REC industry is now full of success stories like these, with many platforms experiencing rapid growth. From their launch in March 2013 to October 2013, Realty Mogul's cumulative investments rose from under $2 million to $8.07 million, with 23 properties under their belt. As of October 2015, they have now financed over 265 properties valued at over $600 million. One of Realty Mogul's most recently funded projects, a medical office building in Hollywood, raised over $8.3 million!

Early on, there was a lot of doubt from real estate professionals as to whether or not the real estate crowdfunding business model would work out. Would investors and sponsors actually make transactions online? While we still can't predict what will happen in the long term, more institutional investors have been embracing the platform and large developers are launching high profile projects on these platforms. Just look at Fundrise's offering for 3 World Trade Center, which recently raised $2 million from accredited investors.

According to Bruce Lipnick, the Founder and CEO of Crowd Alliance, there is also a lot of future potential in the equity crowdfunding market, "In 2013, there were 8.6 million accredited investors including angels that invested a total of $24.8 billion. In 2012, a mere 4 percent of that number, 265,000 business angels, invested $22.5 billion. I see this freedom to advertise private offerings under the Reg D 506c Act, passed 23 September 2013, as the future of opportunities."

Now that Title III of the JOBS Act passed in October 2015 and unaccredited investors will soon be able to be more active in the equity crowdfunding industry, it looks like the industry's progression will continue. According to Massolution, a crowdfunding research firm, the commercial real estate crowdfunding industry hit $1 billion in 2014, was expected to grow to more than $2.5 billion in 2015 and may exceed $250 billion in 2020!

Top Real Estate Crowdfunding Projects in 2014

17 John Street – New York

Platform: Prodigy Network

Amount Raised: $85.3M ($25M crowdfunded)

Closed: September 2014

The initial crowdfunding campaign for 17 John Street helped raise funds for the building's purchase in August. The building, which is only one block away from the World Trade Center, is now being converted into an extended stay hotel. Prodigy Network is currently looking to raise another $70 million to add a glass addition to the building.

Cumberland Metro – Illinois

Platform: Realty Mogul

Amount Raised: $18.5M

Closed: November 2014

This campaign raised money for a large office park acquisition by Brennan Investment Group. The complex is made up of 12 single story-buildings near the Chicago O'Hare International Airport. Brennan Group is now in charge of implementing property management, a leasing program, and making improvements to the property.

90-94 Fulton Street – New York

Platform: iFunding

Amount Raised: $250M ($8M crowdfunded)

Closed: January 2014

Mavrix Group will be the developer for the new condo towers going up at 90-94 Fulton Street. This project is notable because it is not only iFunding's largest project to date, but also their first in New York. The tower is expected to be as large as 250,000 square feet and approximately 75 stories.

Parc Bordeaux Apartments – Indiana

Platform: Realty Mogul

Amount Raised: $8.7M

Closed: December 2014

Parc Bordeaux Apartments is a multi-family property that raised funds in exchange for equity on Realty Mogul. Minimum investments on Realty Mogul start from $5,000.

AKA United Nations – New York

Platform: Prodigy Network

Amount Raised: $68.5M ($10M crowdfunded)

Closed: September 2014

The AKA United Nations raise was a joint venture between Prodigy Network and Korman Communities. They will be renovating the 95 unit, 20 story building at 234 East 46th Street that consists of luxury furnished residences, a lobby lounge, health and fitness center, conference area, and more.

Hamptons Luxury Waterfront Residence – New York

Platform: Fundrise

Amount Raised: $1M

Closed: September 2014

This was Fundrise's first investment in the Hamptons. This property was under construction with real estate development company, Chatham Development, and the platform expects it to attract luxury homebuyers.

Plaza at Riverlakes – California

Platform: Realty Mogul

Amount Raised: $17.3M

Closed: December 2014

Plaza at Riverlakes was an equity purchase for a retail shopping center in Bakersfield.

Mainstreet Bloomington – Indiana

Platform: CrowdStreet

Amount Raised: $1.6M

Closed: July 2014

Mainstreet Bloomington is a new senior care development project by Mainstreet, a company that develops short-stay rehabilitation centers and long-term care properties. The project raised $1.6 million in a four week period, a record for crowdfunding in health care real estate. Investors are expected to earn a 14 percent annualized yield.

290 and 294 Harman Street – New York

Platform: Fundrise

Amount Raised: $1.8M

Closed: October 2014

This Fundrise project was for a multi-family property that was acquired by Cayuga Capital Management. The plan was to renovate the four adjacent apartment buildings to bring rent up to market price.

Lakeside at Town Center Apts – Georgia

Platform: Realty Mogul

Amount Raised: $38.2M

Closed: October 2014

Lakeside at Town Center is a 358 unit apartment including a tennis court, playground, fitness center, and more. The deal was sponsored by Arenda Capital Management, and according to Realty Mogul's CEO, it is the first 'Class A' property they have funded.

Who Are The Major Players Out There?

Fundrise: Fundrise is an online investment platform that allows you to invest in individual commercial real estate. It features both public offerings available to local investors and private offerings available to accredited investors. Fundrise offerings provide shares of equity ownership in specific properties. Their fee is 0-3%.

According to the Washington Post, "Developers have used the platform to close investments for more than a dozen projects totaling more than $10 million. Money is currently being raised for four projects, in Austin, Texas; San Francisco; Philadelphia and Brooklyn, N.Y. When those projects close, the total raised through Fundrise could top $12 million"

Realty Mogul: With the tagline, "Invest with as little as $5,000," Realty Mogul is one of the top crowdfunding platforms for real estate. It serves as a marketplace for accredited investors to pool money online and buy shares of pre-screened real estate investments. The platform offers the opportunity to browse cash-flowing equity investments and real estate loans. Should you chose to invest, there is a fee associated with each investment. The fees depend on the type of investment (loan purchase or equity purchase) and the nature of the transaction.

RealtyShares: RealtyShares is an online investment platform that uses crowdfunding to pool investors into private real estate investments. Accredited Investor members have access to extensive information on a variety of investment properties and can invest as little as $5000 into each such property. Some of the real estate asset classes, including: Residential, Commercial, Retail and Mixed-Use.

The website states, "There are absolutely no fees to investors for our current first position loan offerings. Rather, we charge the borrower listing and related fees to cover our costs."

Fun fact: They accept Bitcoins!

CrowdStreet: CrowdStreet is a fundraising platform connecting accredited investors with professionally-managed real estate investments. CrowdStreet features both equity and debt investment opportunities, including multifamily, retail, office, industrial and land opportunities. In addition to traditional direct investments,

Like the other real estate crowdfunding sites, CrowdStreet explains, "No. There are no investor fees for joining CrowdStreet and accessing the investment opportunities."

GroundBreaker: GroundBreaker provides technology for deal sponsors and developers. "Connect with your investor network and grow it organically. When ready, raise capital directly from your investors and close your deals online. Post-closing we give you a toolset so you can manage your investor reporting and distributions." GroundBreaker charges sponsors a flat monthly fee for the use of its platform. Investors pay nothing.

Patch of Land: Patch of Land lets accredited investors invest in real estate opportunities online, like a loan purchase for a residential fix and flip. "In this investment, investors pool their money to buy a loan. The loan is tied to a residential property that is being rehabilitated and the property is intended to be sold directly after rehabilitation."

There is also the ability to invest in an equity purchase for commercial buy and hold, where investors pool their money to purchase a piece of a specific commercial property. That property is acquired and managed by a professional investment company with a track record of success.

How do the major platforms differ?

Some real estate investments are structured using LLCs where the platform deals exclusively with the sponsor. Sponsors may put in 5-20% to align their interests with investors, limited members (the smaller investors in the deal) could provide up to 95% of the capital. For this, they may receive a preferred return on their investment and share in other cash flow or profits. They may also get tax benefits. With other real estate investments, you'll be dealing directly with the sponsor and the crowdfunding platform will simply enable the transaction to take place.

Where the book goes from here

I hope you're as excited as I am about the growing real estate crowdfunding industry! In the rest of this book, we're going to further demystify this new investment opportunity and share some tips for investors and sponsors.

Chapter 2: The Regulatory Environment

The JOBS Act was passed by President Obama in 2012 to help encourage the creation of new jobs by reducing SEC regulations on general solicitation for small businesses. The SEC explains, "The Act requires the SEC to write rules and issue studies on capital formation, disclosure and registration requirements." In the four years that have followed, the SEC has reduced some of the obstacles that companies face when looking to raise capital.

Before then, the concept of real estate crowdfunding seemed far out of reach, although early innovators in a number of industries saw its potential. With the help of the internet and early crowdfunding platforms, regulators are finally starting to accept this new method of selling and managing securities as a solution to the real estate funding gap.

This does not mean that it has been smooth sailing so far. There have been as many criticisms of the SEC's choices over the past few years as there have been fans. In spite of several delays, Titles II and III of the JOBS Act, along with Regulation A+, have been passed. This gives both accredited and unaccredited investors an unprecedented opportunity to take part in online equity and debt investments, including investing in real estate in their own neighborhood and beyond.

In this chapter you will learn about how the new SEC regulations will have an effect on real estate crowdfunding platforms, sponsors and investors.

Regulations for Crowdfunding Platforms

Title II Rules – Accredited Investors: Title II of the JOBS Act went into effect on September 23 2013. Under this law, REC platforms have two options when dealing with individual accredited investors, 506(b) offerings and 506(c) offerings.

506(b) offerings: General solicitation is not allowed for 506b offerings. This means that as a platform, you can't publicly advertise specific projects, but you are allowed to advertise your platform. These include sponsored ads on social media, like Facebook, for example.

After learning about one of these platforms, accredited investors can sign up and self-identify their income or net worth. In this case, a platform is required by the SEC to have an existing relationship with investors or they must impose a 30-day cooling-off period before a new investor can take part in any offerings.

506(c) offerings: General solicitation is allowed for 506c offerings, meaning that platforms can advertise specific opportunities to the public, However, investors cannot self-certify. Before accepting investments, platforms must take reasonable steps to verify an investor's accredited status, which can be done by requesting documents like tax returns or bank statements.

Platforms who do not follow SEC and FINRA (Financial Industry Regulatory Authority) guidelines can be investigated, fined, and even shut down.

Title III Rules – Unaccredited Investors: Title III of the JOBS Act was passed in October 2015. These rules are supposed to go into effect in 2016, allowing unaccredited investors the chance to take part in securities offerings online. Platforms will finally have access to this huge new investor base, but they will have some big choices to make. Title III involves even more rules and regulators expect platforms to maintain the same high standards as always.

To make offerings under Title III you must first be registered as a broker-dealer or portal intermediary. Platforms using Title III to conduct online real estate offerings are also required to provide educational materials that explain to the public what the risks are and how these deals work. Platforms must also take action and use preventative measures against fraud – one of the things that previously destroyed the open REC market.

In addition to enabling the sale of securities online, platforms are also required to give investors information about sponsors and offerings and provide in-platform communication channels allowing investors and sponsors to discuss offerings.

Platforms are not allowed to offer advice or recommendations to investors. They are also restricted from soliciting sales on the platform and compensating or restricting others from soliciting. Platforms cannot hold, possess or handle investor funds or securities.

Regulation A+ Rules: While the cost of issuing a Regulation A+ offering has deterred many from giving it a try, several REC platforms have experimented with using Regulation A+ as a way to include unaccredited investors in real estate deals.

Tier 1: Since Tier 1 deals are affected by State Registration rules, platforms that choose this option need to be careful where they operate. These Regulation A+ deals may be limited to only a select few states.

Tier 2: State Registration is not required for Tier II offerings, so more states can take part in these offerings.

Regulations for Sponsors

Title II Rules – Accredited Investors: Sponsors can take advantage of Title II of the JOBS Act to raise funds from accredited investors by filing a Form D with the SEC. This exemption gives small businesses an opportunity to sell securities to accredited investors without the same amount of time, disclosures and expense that is required of companies going public (like in an IPO). You can even get started today if you want to!

Title II is convenient because it lets you raise money through either equity or debt deals and there is no maximum amount of capital that you can raise. If you choose to raise capital this way, you also don't have to submit to an SEC review or provide annual audits or financial reports.

506b offerings: 506b offerings let you raise investments from up to 35 unaccredited investors. State Registration is required. There is no general solicitation allowed for these offerings.

506c offerings: You are not allowed to raise money from unaccredited investors when making a 506c offering, and State Registration may or may not be required. General solicitation is allowed for 506c offerings.

Title III Rules – Unaccredited Investors: Title III of the JOBS Act is expected to go into effect in early 2016, allowing startups and small businesses to raise up to $1 million per year – and finally that will include investments from unaccredited investors.

As usual, there are still going to be restrictions on how much an individual can invest (more on that later). Sponsors must make these offerings through a Broker Dealer or Registered Funding Platform. Unlike some of the options we have already discussed, a Title III offering will require more disclosures, including a 21-day SEC review and annual financial reports/audits.

The SEC will need information about owners of 20% or more of the company, directors and other high-level staff. Sponsors must provide a description of the business and where the funds will be used. The company must also provide independently audited financial statements.

Regulation A+ Rules: Unlike Title II offerings, Regulation A+ offerings can only be made after being published in the Federal Register for 60 days. Unaccredited investors are allowed to take part in both of these offerings, but they can only invest up to 10%

of their annual income or net worth. Accredited investors can self-certify for Regulation A+ deals. General solicitation is also allowed.

Regulation A+ is the only SEC exemption that requires you to actually register with the SEC, making it like a mini-IPO. Whereas Title II and Title III are good for seed and scale as well as growth stages, Regulation A+ deals are the most expensive to issue and are best for entrepreneurs looking to fund their growth stages.

According to Crowd Expert, "Fundrise, EarlyShares, and GroundFloor are real estate investment crowdfunding platforms to keep an eye on, as they have expressed interest in utilizing Reg A+ to make offerings available to unaccredited investors."

Tier 1: With this type of offering, you are allowed to raise under $20 million and State Registration is required. Tier 1 offerings don't need annual financial reports or get an SEC review but there is a Cooperative Review by NASAA.

Tier 2: With this type of offering, you are allowed to raise up to $50 million and State Registration is not required. For Tier 2 offerings there will be an SEC review and yearly audits/financial reports.

Regulations for Investors

Title II Rules – Accredited Investors: To invest in a 506b or 506c deal under Title II of the JOBS Act, you are required to be an accredited investor (although issuers can include up to 35 unaccredited investors in the deal). This means having a net worth of $1 million, excluding your primary residence, or an income of over $200K ($300K for couples).

While some platforms using 506c rules are required to verify investors' accredited status, those that use 506b can allow investors to self-certify as accredited.

Title III Rules – Unaccredited Investors: The amounts that accredited investors will be able to invest in REC projects when

Title III goes into effect are as follows: those who make less than $100K a year can invest $2,000 or 5% of their annual income. Investors who make over $100K per year can invest up to 10% of their annual income.

Regulation A+ Rules: Unaccredited investors can take part in both Tier 1 and Tier 2 versions of Regulation A+, as long as their investment does not exceed 10% of their annual income or net worth. Accredited investors who want to take part in a Regulation A+ offering can self-certify.

Thoughts on the Future of the REC Regulatory Environment

The future of real estate crowdfunding and the successful adoption of these new regulations depend on a few different factors. The two major ones that come to mind are education and fraud.

Now that unaccredited investors will once again be able to take part in equity investments, educating them on the risks and smartest ways to invest is going to be key. One of the big reasons that unaccredited investors haven't been able to participate in these kinds of deals for the past 80 years is because they lacked the proper knowledge and investing experience, or an easy way to learn more.

The internet and crowdfunding have paved the way for the JOBS Act and all of the changes that have come along with it. By bringing most of the paperwork and process online, saving time and money, and reducing regulations that have been discouraging small businesses from seeking funding, it seems as though this model could work out well.

Businesses still have some hoops to jump through in order to make these kinds of offerings though, in the form of disclosures and other costs associated with running these kinds of campaigns (which can run you anywhere from $5K to $150K).

Another potential wrench in these new regulations is the possibility of fraud. New investors don't know much about how to avoid fraud. If fraud did become common on these platforms and investors did not take the risks of these investments seriously, stricter rules protecting investors could be reinstated.

Luckily, there are plenty of places where investors can learn how to do proper due diligence before putting their money in a REC deal. Platforms are also required to educate investors and help prevent fraud, some even helping by selectively curating the projects that they host on their platform themselves.

Judging from what crowdfunding has achieved so far, it seems like Regulation A+, and Titles II and III of the JOBS Act are here to stay. The next few years should be exciting ones for the crowdfunding industry, specifically the booming real estate crowdfunding market.

Chapter 3: Real Estate Crowdfunding Tips for Investors

With the invention of real estate crowdfunding and portals that facilitate it, investing in real estate has become easier than ever. Ever since some of the bans on general solicitation having been lifted, it's become super simple for ordinary investors to learn about real estate crowdfunding, see how it works, and ultimately earn passive income through these types of investments.

There are a lot of advantages to investing in real estate under the JOBS Act crowdfunding exemptions. For example, you can now invest smaller amounts in a real estate opportunity alongside other investors (think $5,000), rather than taking on a huge investment by yourself. Also, you can easily create a well-diversified investment portfolio. REC has certainly made this asset class more accessible for accredited investors. Soon, unaccredited investors will also be able to take part in REC deals.

We believe that REC is a good investment option if you don't have the time or want the responsibility of managing a physical property, but you still want to experience the returns that come from partnering with an experienced sponsor. However, naturally, REC is not a great option if you'd like to have 100% control over your investment and take part in day-to-day property operations and management decision making.

As an investor, you need to remember that even with REC there is always risk involved. Minimum investments can still be as high as $1,000 to $5,000 on some platforms, and returns often average at around 12-14%. With REC investments you have very little input or control and there isn't much liquidity in terms of secondary markets where you can sell your investments.

Although there are a lot of great benefits to investing in real estate, we believe that education is still an issue for a lot of investors. Just because you hear about a deal that is supposedly "awesome" doesn't mean it's a great opportunity. Make sure you treat any investment you make as a business decision and consider all of the ins and outs before investing. Also, be sure that you don't invest more than you can handle. This is one of the reasons that some of the rules surrounding investing exist in the first place.

Choosing the right platform

As we mentioned in Chapter 1, there are a few different types of REC platforms. One of the main differences between the platforms we've talked about so far is whether or not they use direct or indirect business models. In the former case, the portal acts as a facilitator between investors and sponsors, meaning that investors get to stay in contact with sponsors throughout the project. In the latter case, portals raise money from sponsors to invest in the deals themselves, and investors don't get the opportunity to reach out to sponsors. This last option comes with some downsides, because the success of your investment is related to how well the REC platform is doing.

Another difference that investors should be aware of is that there are curated and uncurated platforms. Curated platforms are responsible for vetting and underwriting deals, and making sure that the risk is very clear to investors. Uncurated platforms leave most of the due diligence up to investors. Uncurated platforms give you the chance to invest alongside larger investors, but sponsors use templates to fill out information and you must verify most of the claims yourself.

There is absolutely no rush to start investing in this asset class. It's true that smart investors will get in early, but don't sacrifice diligence for speed. We can't recommend a specific REC platform for your investing needs, because every investor is different, but we consider the websites in Chapter 1 to be a good list of platforms to consider.

You're going to need to spend some time getting to know these platforms and familiarize yourself with the different marketplaces before you commit yourself to an investment decision. Just remember that while it's true that great technology and customer service can make your investments easier to manage, at the end of the day, your performance will simply depend on the individual investments themselves.

Most popular types of REC investments

Cash flowing properties are the most common and least risky types of REC investments available through REC. It is rare to see REC platforms that deal with new developments, because it is harder to judge whether or not those will be successful and earn the expected returns for investors.

Keep in mind that what might be a great investment for a friend or colleague of yours might not be right for you. Everyone should establish their own unique investment criteria based on the risk they are comfortable with and their end goals.

That being said, sponsors and investors have seen success in properties such as senior housing, medical office space and apartments. Retail investments and other commercial real estate can be great, but it is important to take into account things like location, visibility, population growth and diversity, and income levels. Office property is also popular, although losing a tenant can affect returns. Multi-family residential properties offer some of the most stable returns, and the loss of a single family has little impact.

One of the growing asset classes that we've seen in the last few years has been the emergence of debt-based fixed income investment opportunities, like those offered by Fundrise and Patch of Land, which are referred to at peer to peer lending investments. Fundrise has also made available an "eREIT" which is an alternative to a standard REIT, with lower fees. The eREIT focuses on fixed income debt investments.

How to stay protected and avoid fraud

One of the biggest challenges of REC is to educate the population about these great new investment opportunities while effectively communicating the risk involved. Investors need to be ready to do due diligence before coming to a decision, including: getting legal advice and making sure that they are dealing with sponsors who have a proven track record.

The highest quality platforms and sponsors make all of the information you need to make a good investment decision transparent and easy to understand. So far it seems like users are taking their time after joining these platforms before jumping into any investments, which suggests that they understand the risks involved and want to make sure that REC is not too good to be true.

At the same time, you should go to lengths to do your own research. Don't simply rely on the research team of the REC platform or the "social proof" given by other investors.

The number of years a sponsor has been in business, how many deals they have done and the money they have transacted all point towards their track record and whether or not investing with them is a good choice. Inexperienced investors may not have what it takes to manage a property well or may not have values that are aligned with their investors, meaning your money is likely more at risk with them.

Personally, we believe that three of the biggest risks for real estate crowdfunding investors are the concepts of "social proof," "urgency," and "expert authority." Although these are effective mechanisms to sell investments on behalf of the actual REC website and the sponsor, they can lead to unwise choices for investors.

Just because a deal has a great number of investors or talented investors with a proven track record does NOT mean that it is a good deal. There are countless examples of smart, educated, "proven" investors going belly up on deals throughout their career. In addition, you can be a complete fool and still make money in a bull market. Social proof is a good filter that you can use to pay attention to certain deals, but don't use it as the deciding factor. Do your own research and come to your own conclusions. Don't let your emotions crowd out logic.

Second, the fact that there is a limited time to get in on a REC investment often times will create a sense of urgency, which can crowd out logical judgements. While you should get to work as soon as possible when evaluating a deal, try to adopt the mindset that you have as much time in the world to make this decision. Remember that these investments are illiquid, so you be will faced with the positive or negative consequences of your decision for some time to come.

Finally, since the REC platform often times serves as the deal making middleman who may have curated these specific opportunities, it's easy to assign a status of "expert" to their team and marketplace. It's also easy to assume that the actual platform has far more knowledge than you do about real estate investing and crowdfunding in general. Sometimes, this is an acceptable assumption to make, but other times, it can lead to poor investment decisions simply because you were subtly influenced by the opinions or passive suggestions of an individual or team with "expert" status.

Diversifying your investments

When deciding what types of REC investments you want to make, you will have to decide what risk levels you are comfortable with (these can always change as you gain more experience). Low risk investments are safer but offer low returns, whereas high risk investments often lead to higher returns if things go well.

We recommend budgeting time and money to learn the ins and outs of investing in REC on various platforms before you really commit yourself to this new asset class. By setting aside a bit of money specifically for the purpose of testing, any mistakes that you make will be an acceptable part of the learning process.

With a greater understanding of how REC works, you can build a diversified real estate portfolio. Diversifying helps mitigate risk by including a mixture of high, medium and low risk investments in your portfolio. This way, if one type of investment doesn't earn the returns you expect, your portfolio can still make a positive return.

One example of this is how many people start with residential investments which can offer short investment horizons. As investors become more comfortable and look for growth, commercial properties (which are higher earning and often have long term leases) become their preferred option.

Best places for REC investments

Some experts have found that there are higher return rates in the Mid-West and other less populated markets. Others have found that places like Vegas often have a lot of foreclosures, which opens up a lot of opportunities (as Dolf de Roos explains in 52 Homes in 52 Weeks).

When it comes to real estate investing, investors must also decide between local investments and cross country investments. Both of these options have pros and cons, and like most other things, this depends greatly on the unique circumstances of the investor.

For example, some investors like the idea of investing in their own communities. In this way, they can 'own' a part of where they live. Their investments become a source of pride as well as a source of income. There are platforms, like Fundrise, that are built specifically around these ideas and others that operate in specific states only.

Some platforms, on the other hand, are focused on facilitating REC opportunities on a global level. These platforms allow even international investors to participate in deals, and encourage investors from anywhere to participate in large investments. These investments are common, but might be best for investors who want to silently participate in a deal and don't feel the need to be close to the property to invest confidently.

Chapter 4: Real Estate Crowdfunding Tips for Sponsors

REC opens up a lot of opportunities for everyone involved, including investors who never had access to these kinds of real estate investments in the past, platforms who benefit from simplifying the investing process, and sponsors, who get to raise investments faster than ever before.

Capital isn't being provided efficiently by banks, and a lot of projects that are doing great in the REC arena would probably have never achieved the funding they needed without this new, alternative method. Software is giving sponsors new ways of accessing stable funding in less time with fewer fees. Crowdfunding your real estate investments also becomes a huge advantage over time. As you complete more projects and get media coverage, your deals get funded faster.

This guide will give you information about the requirements that are needed to sponsor a REC project, the types of platforms out there, and how to get started. The best part is that once your first project is successfully funded it becomes much easier to launch another one.

Since general solicitation bans have been lifted, sponsors now have the chance to build an online brand for themselves and investors can familiarize themselves with sponsors who have a proven track record for success. If you're looking to do a high volume of deals, REC is probably the best option for you.

What type of platform is best for sponsors?

Crowdfunding allows you to reduce the amount of funding that you need to raise from your own professional network for a new real estate deal. Some REC platforms will even pre-fund your deal with their own money, because they are confident in you, the deal, and the investors that they have backing projects on their platform.

The type of platform a sponsor chooses can have a lot to do with their success, and each type of platform has its own strengths and drawbacks.

Crowdstreet, for example, is an online intermediary providing sponsors with a direct relationship to investors and the option to use a white label platform to host your offering on your own website. Other platforms, like Fundrise, take a more indirect approach with investors by forming an LLC and pooling investors' money to make one investment. In this case, the platform becomes an investment manager, keeps contact with sponsors and passes information along to investors. These platforms generally charge additional fees for acting as the investment manager.

Different platforms also have different requirements for sponsors they are willing to work with. Whereas Crowdstreet takes a more experience-based approach and works with sponsors with a lot of experience, other platforms may be more likely to give newer sponsors a chance (assuming they pass the required background checks, show that they can manage the property and the deal is a sound one).

Other things to consider when looking into the pros and cons of different REC platforms include partnerships with or the presence of institutional investors on the platform, which is good for ensuring stable capital.

Choosing between platforms that operate under different crowdfunding exemptions really depends on your preference and the level of reporting and disclosures that you are comfortable with. While some platforms (like RealtyShares) have so far opted to run as a 506(b) platform to avoid burdens of having to verify investor's accredited status, some say that if you want to reach a wider audience, then general solicitation, meaning 506(c) platforms, are the way. Still, many of RealtyShares deals are funded in under 24 hours and they have a 98% success rate, which suggests that investors are learning about REC without the additional advertising.

Types of properties that make good REC Investments

There are a lot of factors that go into deciding whether or not a proposed REC project is approved. So far, REC platforms do not deal with new developments. Instead, they prefer to deal with income-earning property that they are confident will achieve relatively quick returns for investors.

This means projects like fix and flip, multi-family residential properties, office, industrial, retail properties and more. When looking into a deal you have to be aware of all of the possible factors that could affect it, like the area that the property is in, population, etc.

If you are an experienced sponsor and the first deal that you bring to a REC platform is denied, don't give up. There can be small reasons that a deal is not good for REC but as you propose more deals you will start to see which ones are a better fit and why.

One example of a deal that did well in 2014 is Cumberland Metro, in Illinois. The project raised $18.5 million on Realty Mogul for a large office park acquisition by Brennan Investment Group. The complex is made up of 12 single story-buildings near the Chicago O'Hare International Airport (a great location!). Brennan Group is now in charge of implementing property management, a leasing program, and making improvements to the property.

Getting Started

Once you have chosen the right platform for you, looked up deals in your area of interest and are ready to continue, all you have to do is follow a few simple steps to get started. The great thing about REC is that you bring the expertise when it comes to managing the property, while the platforms do a lot to help educate you and make sure you have everything else you will need.

One of the first things you will need to do is create a profile and enter in some basic information about yourself and the deal you want to get funding for. Next, the platform generally reaches out to you to get more details and answer any of your questions. Once they have done the required due diligence (the time for this can vary depending on the type of platform), the underwriting and finalizing of the deal takes place and the project is posted on the platform for investors to see.

Requirements

While the general requirements to become a sponsor vary from platform to platform, one of the most important things REC platforms look for is a track record owning and operating real estate assets. Many platforms require sponsors to have anywhere from 5-10+ years of experience, and the more successful projects under your belt, the better. As part of their due diligence, most platforms look for sponsors with no bankruptcies, past foreclosures, criminal activity, good credit, detailed plans with projections, etc.

When it comes to requirements (whether it's the platform, the SEC, or any other regulations that you need to follow) the best thing to do is make sure you research and know the rules beforehand. One of the best ways to do this is to connect with portals and other industry professionals. Generally, they will have a lot of expertise and knowledge in the area and consider it part of their mission to share their wisdom with others.

Even though REC will play a big role in connecting you to new investors, you still need to develop your social networks and bring in some of the capital yourself.

Best Practices

People currently feel disconnected from their investments, but the new transparency associated with crowdfunding can give you an opportunity to increase their interest. Since this is still a growing industry, getting in early and building your reputation can have big future advantages.

Before getting involved in a deal, make sure you ask yourself these important questions, like can you afford it? Not only acquiring the property itself but upkeep, tax, insurance, and the potential for other unforeseen circumstances to lower property values, etc. Keep an eye out for areas with a lot of potential and talk to other investors, lenders, and repair service providers to learn as much about the market as you can. Luckily, if you're an experienced real estate manager, this area should be the easiest for you.

You must build an open and honest relationship with the platform you are using. Keep in mind that the closer you work with them (and get all of the necessary documents submitted) the faster your deal will be funded.

It is recommended that you give investors as much information about the deal as possible. A two-page deal has very little detail compared to a 20+ page deal, and that detail can be the difference between deciding to invest in you or another sponsor. With REC, sponsors have the opportunity to make investors feel special, because they know exactly what property they are investing in and the vision behind it. Sharing updates throughout your project and earning the expected returns can have a big impact when it comes to an investor's decision to back another one of your projects in the future.

Chapter 5: Industry Leaders Weigh In

Today's industry leaders are REC's pioneers. These dedicated men and women have a vision of what the real estate industry could look like and have believed in it when very few people thought it was possible to take this industry to the web. CrowdCrux asked some CEOs and leaders of today's top REC platforms a few questions about their platforms and where the industry is going. Here is what they had to say:

CrowdStreet co-founders Tore Steen and Darren Powderly

What laws/exemptions does your platform operate under and why?

"CrowdStreet currently operates under several laws/exemptions including:

Reg. D Section 506b - Sponsors using our Sponsor Direct SaaS solution to publish investment offerings to their own websites typically do so under the 506b exemption of US securities code. Sponsor Direct allows real estate operating companies to easily publish and promote offerings to their existing networks of investors and manage the resulting online funding events and communications.

Reg. D Section 506c - Sponsors publishing investment offerings to our direct-to-investor public Marketplace do so under the 506c exemption of the US securities code. Utilizing the 506c exemption enables the real estate operating company to generally solicit their offerings through the CrowdStreet Marketplace to reach a new audience of investors and directly acquire new investors for their businesses - something that is not possible with the SPV marketplace model used by nearly every other crowdfunding real estate marketplace."

Will the platform be allowing more unaccredited investors when Title III of the Jobs Act goes into effect?

"CrowdStreet is monitoring Title III but we do not currently have immediate plans to market a Title III offering when it goes into effect in May of 2016. We are however, cautiously optimistic that Title III will ultimately have a role in online commercial real estate syndication."

Do you have any advice for sponsors and investors?

"Not all crowdfunding platforms are created equal. For those investors interested in investing in private real estate offerings via an online platform, they should research several of the leading platforms that are committed to investor protection through best practices in the areas of sponsorship quality, property quality, professionally prepared offering documents, investor accreditation, website functionality and security.

• CrowdStreet's marketplace serves as an intermediary connecting accredited investors with pre-approved real estate sponsors.

• Be careful of platforms without pre-qualifying standards.

• Investors should have a clear understanding of the financial engineering of an offering and know exactly where their investment is in the capital sources of a particular property.

• Crowdfunding is a highly regulated industry, so investors should seek to understand how the platform achieves regulatory compliance."

Does CrowdStreet only do equity deals? If so - why is your focus on equity rather than debt, or both?

"The CrowdStreet Marketplace offers the following types of real estate investment structures:

1. Equity, which is often referred to as "joint venture equity"

2. Preferred equity

3. Mezzanine Debt (debt that is subordinate to the senior loan)

4. Senior debt (typically offered via a fund structure)

It is important to note that, because the CrowdStreet Marketplace offers investors the ability to invest directly with an operating company, any debt investments will be offered and managed by a lender. For this reason and for additional reasons inherent to the direct-to-operator approach, the majority of investment opportunities on the CrowdStreet Marketplace are structured as equity or preferred equity."

Do you have any tips for investors on the best types of properties or what to look for when deciding if a deal is right for them?

"Investors should be equipped with the proper set of tools to evaluate risk when contemplating a commercial real estate investment. The detail page of offerings on the CrowdStreet Marketplace contain the following types of information, all of which are intended to allow investors to examine all aspects of an investment opportunity and make informed decisions:

1. Quality of Sponsorship - CrowdStreet believes that good commercial real estate investments stem from high quality real estate operators. Therefore, a recommended starting point when evaluating an investment opportunity is to analyze the investment manager. The company's website is a good place to begin and things to look for include: 1) depth and breadth of leadership team experience 2) track record and 3) investment product alignment with experience and expertise.

2. Structure - In general, the higher the position of the investment in the capital stack, the more risk the investor assumes. This is why a lender may offer senior debt at 70% of loan-to-value on a property at a 5% interest rate while the equity investors that comprise the remaining 30% of the capital expect annualized returns of 15% or greater. Therefore, a good place for an investor to start when thinking through an investment is to decide if he/she is willing to accept "first dollar loss risk" in a property in exchange for the potential of solid double digit annualized returns or instead, seek an investment at a lower position in a capital stack (such as preferred equity or mezzanine debt) and accept single-digit to low double digit annualized returns.

3. Location - Instead of the simple adages often applied to the importance of real estate location, we feel that an investor can benefit by thinking through location by asking him/herself the following question, "will the physical asset remain relevant at this location and in its current format for the duration of the intended holding period?". For example, redevelopment opportunities are intended to cure an irrelevant format while arguing that the location is still relevant and will remain so indefinitely. From a macroeconomic perspective, consider factors such as job growth, population growth, population migration and infrastructure development trends. Knowing where people live and work in the asset's metro area and where people will increasingly (or decreasingly) live and work in the future are important considerations when making a real estate investment decision."

What makes CrowdStreet the best option for sponsors?

"1. Direct-to-Investor vs. SPV marketplace

The CrowdStreet Marketplace is exceptional among real estate crowdfunding marketplaces. Nearly all of our competitors use what's called a special-purpose vehicle or "SPV" funding structure for their marketplaces.

The SPV funding structure creates a separate legal entity for every investment offering, which is used to collect and then later disperse the investments made by participating investors. While the SPV structure simplifies administration of the funding event, it has very significant downside for the sponsor - the sponsor doesn't actually acquire any new investors for their business. All sponsors receive at the end of the process is a check from SPV #123, LLC. - they have no information on who the individual investors are who contributed to their offering.

Compare this with CrowdStreet's Direct-to-Investor marketplace model. CrowdStreet provide a software solution that allows sponsors to achieve the same funding goals as SPV marketplace models while at the same time enabling them to actually acquire new investors for their business. At the end of the process the CrowdStreet system electronically registers payment and creates a database profile for each individual investor. The sponsor now owns these investor records and can use them to promote subsequent 506b or 506c investment offerings.

2. Full Investor Acquisition and Management Solution

What really makes CrowdStreet the best option for sponsors is our comprehensive solution for investor acquisition and management, The CrowdStreet Platform. Currently the CrowdStreet Platform is comprised two components, our public Marketplace and our SaaS-based solution Sponsor Direct. Using the CrowdStreet Platform sponsors can manage every aspect of CRE investor acquisition, management, and conversion:

• Publish + promote investment offerings to existing investor networks

• Publish + promote investment offerings to public marketplaces

• Nurture prospects via secure + auditable communications with potential investors

• Close deals faster with a fully online investment document workflow

• Increase investor value with a secure online investor portal (w/ performance reporting & downloadable K-1s)

We have competitors offering point-solutions for the marketplace portion of the Platform (albeit using SPVs instead of direct-to-investor structures), and there are a few companies offering individual components of our SaaS solution such as investor portals or investor-CRM solutions, however there is literally not one competitor offering a comprehensive marketplace + investor acquisition & management solution like what sponsors can achieve with the full CrowdStreet Platform.

Sponsors agree - since we launched the full platform in May 2015 we've added 10 new clients and have scaled to $1 Billion in total asset value posted and $166 Million in total investor funds managed through the platform."

Fundrise CEO & co-founder Ben Miller

"It's been an exciting few years for the investment crowdfunding space with thousands of new companies and investors joining the industry and validating what was once a fringe idea. We are particularly proud of our newest innovation, the Fundrise eREIT, which is available to the public without the costs, middlemen, and inefficiencies of conventional channels. We believe this is a superior alternative to the high fees and volatility of the stock market and a true revolution in how people will invest."

Realty Shares CEO Nav Athwal

What laws/exemptions the platform is operating under and why?

"Real estate crowdfunding is actually a pretty complicated business, because investments are governed by securities laws in addition to the usual real estate considerations. Usually, selling securities to the public requires that a full-blown "registration statement" be filed with the SEC; the primary exemption to that requirement is when investors are limited to those who are "accredited" which means that they satisfy certain net worth or annual income criteria. This exemption -- Rule 506 -- is the one we operate under."

Will you be allowing more unaccredited investors when Title III of the Jobs Act goes into effect?

"We don't have any immediate plans to use Title III, and that's because some of the limitations in Title III make it difficult to use for our real estate platform. We'd only be allowed to raise $1 million annually, and since many of our offerings are that much or more already we'd run into a problem right off the bat. There are also ongoing reporting obligations that would require additional administrative overhead. We continue to look at this area, but for now Title III isn't expected to change our business model."

Do you have any advice for sponsors and investors?

"Crowdfunding sites like RealtyShares are great for sponsors, who can now take advantage of a new source of capital in a way that actually eliminates many of the sponsor's investor relations chores. For investors, real estate crowdfunding has enabled smaller investors to participate in commercial real estate investments that often weren't available to them before.

The great thing about commercial real estate is that it offers a cash flow-oriented investment that often acts as a hedge against inflation. There can also be tax benefits involved with equity investments, particularly when structured with the direct participation vehicles that we use. No investment is guaranteed, of course, but commercial real estate has unique characteristics that argue for its inclusion in an investment portfolio, and crowdfunding has made those investments much more accessible than they used to be."

Chapter 6: The Future of Real Estate Crowdfunding

Real estate is considered to be the largest and most valuable asset class in the US, worth an estimated $40 trillion! There is tremendous potential for the real estate crowdfunding industry. In fact the industry was projected to be worth $2.5 billion in 2015. Joanna Schwartz, CEO of EarlyShares, predicts that this number will likely grow again in 2016. She shared in a company blog post:

"If real estate crowdfunding really did reach $2.57 billion in volume by the close of 2015, as Massolution projected it would, that represents a whopping 150% increase from 2014. That kind of growth is huge, especially for a market as young (and as rapidly evolving) as real estate crowdfunding ... Should 2016 see real estate crowdfunding charge ahead at a similar pace, the market will hit the $3.5 billion mark by the end of 2016. And it may reach even higher heights, thanks to the incorporation of non-accredited investors to the playing field and the rise of new, growth-generating trends across the real estate investing market."

Real estate crowdfunding gives sponsors access capital with less overhead costs, unheard of opportunities to expand their network, and the ability to earn a steady stream of investments for different properties. Once a sponsor is approved and shows that they are capable of running a first successful project, the REC platform they choose can become a valuable partner that support long term funding and growth.

Things We Can Expect

As more people become educated about real estate crowdfunding and the practice starts to become mainstream, more and more investors will join in to participate in deals that they'd never have access to before. Pre-vetted deals mean you don't need the same amount of experience with investing in real estate as was required of investors in the past. Although you still need to think each deal through carefully before investing, a lot of the due diligence is already done for you. Once the public trusts that this is a safe way to invest their money we can expect to see many more people diversifying their investment portfolios with real estate crowdfunding.

The growth of REC has also been good for other businesses like FundAmerica and Accredify, who lend their services to platforms and sponsors. These businesses offer services like investor management tools, help with SEC compliance, e-signature assistance, accredited investor confirmations and much more. What does all of this mean? More jobs, increased profits and more tax revenues for states and federal government. These are markers of economic growth that the JOBS Act was intended to spur. One thing is for sure. It's time for some big changes. Banks are losing customers and many of them are currently trying to get up to speed on crowdfunding or they risk falling behind and becoming irrelevant.

Another thing that the REC industry has us looking forward to is more affordable and reliable ways to collect data on the real estate industry. This will allow it to be studied and improved on in a way that wasn't possible before.

While a few main platforms have taken up a large portion of the market share, platforms are still expected to compete for space in this new industry. It is possible that some smaller platforms might come together to avoid being overshadowed by larger ones. More are expected to launch as entrepreneurs continue to expand into newer, more specific market segments.

Once Title III rules go into effect, we can expect to go towards global expansion (some platforms are already working with foreign investors). One example of this is Wealth Migrate, who raised almost four million to expand their real estate crowdfunding platform in 2015 and have offices in South Africa, Shanghai, Singapore, the U.S., the U.K., and Australia.

Demographics also seem to be shifting towards millennial investors who want to find meaningful investments that work for them, as opposed to the disconnected investments of their parents. They have a better understanding of the technology and the principles behind crowdfunding, so for them the choice seems like a no-brainer. It also makes sense that millennials would support the high transparency that these platforms aim for.

Debt vs. Equity

Some estimates show that crowdfunded real estate deals are equity about 80% of the time, and debt 20% of the time. While there are other affordable debt solutions out there, crowdfunding is bringing equity to the average investor in a new way, which is why the first platforms have mainly focused on equity.

Debt has become more popular recently though, in part because debt is repaid before equity. Debt investors don't participate in profits when the company is sold, like equity investors, so for investors, their preference really depends on their risk tolerance. Since the market is currently restricted to mostly accredited investors, it makes sense that they are more likely to find the risk (and benefits) of equity investments attractive. With rules like Regulation A+ that allow for the inclusion of unaccredited investors, that might change. Newer investors are likely to look to debt investments for faster returns and less risk.

Success Rates

Thanks to the pressure from regulatory bodies like the SEC and FINRA, current REC platforms are held to a very high standard. With every new project that is brought to a platform, they are putting their reputation on the line if that deal eventually goes badly. That means rejecting a lot of sponsors who may not be ready

– and it seems that as a result REC has a relatively low risk/default rate compared to other types of crowdfunding.

The failure rate may be low so far, but there is still not a lot of data available because projects can take 3-5 years from start to finish, and this is still a young industry. Maintaining these high standards will depend on the continued support of regulatory bodies and due diligence of platforms.

Even though new crowdfunding laws have come into effect that make it possible to include unaccredited investors and allow platforms to publicly advertise deals, some platforms have been slow to adopt these changes because of costs, burdensome reporting requirements, and more work for the platform when early business models that only include accredited investors are still working.

Chapter 7: Starting Your Own Real Estate Crowdfunding Platform

"The great danger to the consumer is the monopoly -- whether private or governmental. His most effective protection is free competition at home and free trade throughout the world" - Milton Friedman

We're big supporters of the growing real estate crowdfunding industry and we want to see more entrepreneurs get involved! Competition is not only healthy, but it's a necessary part of innovation and progress.

In this section, we're going to talk about ways to go about setting up your own real estate crowdfunding platform. Then I'm going to go into how to rise above the flock and stand out as a real estate crowdfunding site.

White Label Options

After crowdfunding platforms became popular people started thinking, "Why can't I launch a crowdfunding campaign on my own website?" This way, you would save on platform fees, benefit by keeping investors on your own website, and you wouldn't have to worry about your deals getting overshadowed by others on a platform.

Several companies have launched to fill this need, offering end-to-end software solutions to help you start your own crowdfunding platform. This is a great option for real estate firms that already have a pool of offline investors, but want to digitize everything and streamline the process. It is also a way for firms and sponsors to brand themselves and stand out. Along with these white label services, several of the leading REC platforms have also launched their own white label options.

Here is a list of white label platforms to help you get started:

GroundBreaker: GroundBreaker has a fully customizable, white label, front-to-back SaaS solution available for a flat monthly rate in addition to their public platform. With GroundBreaker's white label option, you get to raise funds on your own website with access to GroundBreaker's resources when it comes to important things like compliance, IT, etc.

CrowdStreet: CrowdStreet launched their private white label marketplace in April 2015 to allow sponsors and firms to digitize and simplify the real estate investment process while maintaining their own network of investors. The same tools to manage investor relations are available in the private marketplace. Sponsors can even choose to run campaigns from their website AND in CrowdStreet's public marketplace if they are looking to expand their investor pool.

CrowdEngine: CrowdEngine is a service that offers custom white label crowdfunding portals. With built-in compliance and due diligence, e-signatures, reporting and more, CrowdEngine helps you make sure that all of the important things are taken care of. CrowdEngine is SEC, FINRA, & Broker-Dealer compliant for Reg A, Reg D 506(b) & 506(c), and intrastate funding.

Katipult: Katipult is a white label software platform that focuses on real estate and equity crowdfunding. With Katipult, you get all of the tools you need to efficiently launch and run your own platform. With 8 years' experience working with big brands, this end-to-end service (which is maintained by software support engineers) is a popular choice. Katipult gives you access to automated accreditation, bad actor checks and verification, and more.

Launcht: Launcht is one of the older white label crowdfunding platforms that was founded in 2010. They help businesses, nonprofits, and colleges/universities set up crowdfunding sites.

Pricing information: Setup – $495-$5,995. Ongoing – $295/mo & 1% of all funds raised – $495/mo & 1% of all funds raised.

CrowdfundHQ: CrowdfundHQ is another software solution that you can use to set up your own platform. They serve the business, equity crowdfunding, peer to peer lending, and nonprofit niches.

Crowdfund Connect: Crowdfund Connect provides a white label solution for entrepreneurs looking to set up an equity, rewards-based, or donation-based crowdfunding websites.

Starting a Platform from Scratch

If you want to get into the real estate crowdfunding industry as an enabler, launching a platform to help connect investors and sponsors without these white label options, it takes a lot more time and expertise. SEC compliance is important, and the regulations vary depending on the laws and exemptions that your platform will choose to operate under.

To start your own crowdfunding platform, you will need a lot of passion, a solid business plan, and a strong team with expertise in a number of areas. This includes staff such as: software engineers, operations, accounting, marketing, real estate, and more. You also need to work on your personal networks and make sure that when you do launch your platform there are investors willing to put their money in deals on your platform.

Here are some examples of key elements of a real estate crowdfunding business model. By writing these things down on paper you can really focus your company's mission, keep track of goals and progress, as well as revenue and cost:

Partners: Partners in your real estate crowdfunding platform can include payment and other service providers, real estate investing communities and institutional investors. This can also include influencers are respected and who can help spread the word about your platform to the industry and potential customers.

Key Activities: The typical key activities for real estate crowdfunding platforms include: educating the public, marketing, platform R&D, networking and partnership development. Once your platform has been launched these are some of the key things that will help drive sponsors and investors to your platform and enable you to form long lasting, mutually beneficial relationships with your customers.

Key Resources: Your key resources for your business will be the 1) crowdfunding platform itself, 2) marketing and education – you can produce videos, blog posts and other learning materials to help people familiarize themselves with real estate crowdfunding and how your platform works, and 3) social networks – a great way to promote your new platform online, with the ability to reach specific demographics at a lower cost.

Value Proposition: What is special or appealing about your platform (thinking about both investors and sponsors)? For example, sponsors can reach more investors and earn steady income for new projects, while investors get access to a new asset class, with lower fees and the ability to make more empowering investments. Most real estate crowdfunding platforms also put the focus on how they aim to be transparent, taking out middleman and the added cost and time associated with traditional real estate investing (like REITs). Another focus of REC is that anyone can do it – at least any sponsor with the right track record, along with individual investors.

Customer Relationships: When it comes to your relationship with your customers, your job is to help the customer understand the real estate crowdfunding process. In the case of your sponsors, you'll have to assist in the preparation and launch of the various projects. Most platforms offer campaign advisory and support services, as well as social media support.

Communication Channels: When you are building up your crowdfunding platform, keep in mind these main communication channels that will be key in helping you spread the word and attract new customers. The first is your crowdfunding platform. It should be optimized so that visitors can easily find the information they need. Next are the different social media platforms, word of mouth, partner programs, along with other multimedia options such as livestreams, webinars, podcasts and instructional videos.

Customers: In the case of real estate crowdfunding, there are two sides to the equation, the sponsors and the investors that form the deals that make up your public marketplace. Be sure you are adequately serving each group. Online, your reputation is everything, especially in a newer industry!

Costs: The main costs that you will have to keep track of when launching and running a real estate crowdfunding platform include: platform development and maintenance, staff salaries, marketing and customer education.

Sources of Revenue: Real estate crowdfunding platforms earn revenue mainly through project commissions (usually about 4-7% for successful projects), although there might also be secondary streams of income such as investor fees.

Standing out from the Flock

There are three main ways that I think new real estate crowdfunding platforms can stand out from their competitors and become a leader in this space.

The first way is simple and comes back to a tried a true method that's existed since the dawn of time. You must build strong positive relationships. Not only with your investors and sponsors, but also with the media, service providers, and experts in the industry. We do business and support individuals that we know, like, and trust. No doubt, it's a longterm game, but it's 100% worth it to cultivate great relationships. Rather than thinking about what you want, ask yourself how you can better serve, entertain, or education an individual that you want to win over.

The second way seems easy, but in practice, it's super hard. The one word that sums it up is marketing. But really, I prefer to think of it as storytelling. It's your job to get your story out there in a crowded world and the success stories of your investors and sponsors. At the end of the day, the only thing that matters is mindshare. By this, I mean real estate in the minds of your target audience. When they think of real estate, do they think of your platform? This topic is beyond the scope of this ebook, but we have a lot of free info on our website, CrowdCrux.com.

Finally, the last way to stand out as a leader in this space is to have the best deals. Yes, it's going to take a lot of work to get sponsors on board with great properties, but it's going to take even more work to attract the best investors. The investors that will be regulars on your platform and end up becoming media stories. You have to be extremely passionate about your cause, ridiculously resourceful, and relentless in your work ethic. Real estate crowdfunding is a new industry and this is a land grab. Good luck!

Chapter 8: Conclusion

Personally, I can't wait to share more developments with you in the new and growing real estate crowdfunding industry. I think there is a tremendous amount of opportunity for investors, sponsors, and service providers in this niche. I hope that this ebook got you thinking about how the internet is transforming real estate financing.

Although we have done our best to be thorough, accurate, and comprehensive, I urge you to seek out more information if you're thinking of investing with a REC platform. This is a rapidly changing sector, with many new regulations and practices. Thankfully, we have many free articles and podcasts on CrowdCrux.com to keep you up to date on the industry. I've also set up RealEstateCrowdfundingExplained.com with dedicated resources related to this guide.

If you take one thing away from this ebook, it should be that you NEED to start to pay attention to REC. Now is the time to familiarize yourself with this new sector and get a jump on your competitors and other investors. Often times, when a new industry emerges, it's the participants who get in first that reap the most rewards.

Good luck on your journey!

- Sal & Krystine.

P.S. If you enjoyed this overview, please take a second to leave us a positive review on Amazon! Thanks!

About the Author

Salvador Briggman founded the popular blog, CrowdCrux, which has been cited by the New York Times, The Wallstreet Journal, CNN, and more. He helps entrepreneurs raise money on crowdfunding platforms like Kickstarter and Indiegogo. Last year, he helped nearly 400,000 individuals raise money from the crowd through his website, products, newsletter, and forum.